John Osborne

by

HAROLD FERRAR

 **Columbia University Press**

NEW YORK & LONDON 1973

MBIA ESSAYS ON MODERN WRITERS
ries of critical studies of English,
iental, and other writers whose works are of contemporary
artistic and intellectual significance.

Editor

George Stade

Advisory Editors

Jacques Barzun   W. T. H. Jackson   Joseph A. Mazzeo

John Osborne is Number 67 of the series

HAROLD FERRAR
is Assistant Professor of English
at Columbia University.

Library of Congress Cataloging in Publication Data

Ferrar, Harold.
 John Osborne.
 (Columbia essays on modern writers, no. 67)
 Bibliography: p. 48
 1. Osborne, John, 1929–   I. Series.
PR6029.S39Z635   822'.9'14   72-13527
ISBN 0-231-03361-3

John Osborne

When *Look Back in Anger* opened in London in May of 1956, it was hailed as an overnight revolution in the English theater. John Osborne, a twenty-six-year-old unknown actor and journalist, suddenly became the unwilling father of a "new British drama" and leader in spite of himself of the media-styled Angry Young Man school. In early 1956 this overeager categorization included just two novelists (Kingsley Amis and John Wain) and Osborne. Men of widely divergent backgrounds (Amis and Wain are Oxonians and dons, Osborne a high school dropout), they shared at the time no more than a desire to discredit a suffocating class system, and all resisted assignment to common membership in a literary school. Amis and Wain had written traditionally realistic, even sentimental, picaresque first novels. If we view *Look Back in Anger* in light of the development of drama since Ibsen, Osborne seems as formally conservative as the "angry" novelists. The "revolution" *Anger* led to the barricades of Shaftesbury Avenue was a very specific local rising. Only by placing Osborne's arrival in its immediate social and theatrical contexts can we distinguish the part of his talent that belongs in the realistic tradition of contemporary drama from the political part that administered what John Russell Taylor sees as "the biggest shock to the system of British theater since the advent of Shaw."

Eric Bentley has divided modern drama into two modes, realism and reactions to realism. Realism itself was a revolutionary reaction to the melodramatic sloppiness and mechanistic emptiness of the pseudo-serious Victorian theater—Shaw's Sardoodledom. Long acquaintance with experimental antirealistic

[3]

forms and the current engulfing vogue of absurdism, minimal drama, improvisational drama, and audience participation makes it difficult for us to remember that the realism of the free theater movement was the first "revolution" of modern drama. In fact, the all-out attempt to render domestic environment and individual behavior with maximum likeness to the observed surface of ordinary life is probably the most enduring revolutionary innovation of modern theater, a unique aesthetic product of the liberal democratic imagination. Although fourth-wall realism began to be discredited the morning after it appeared, it rapidly established its dominion. And nearly a century later, a dynamic playwright like Osborne can still be most at home in Ibsen's parlor or not far from it. Osborne's best work is essentially realistic; he has an uncanny and discomforting gift for forcing us to an instantaneous emotional awareness of the closeness of the world of his plays to middle-class urban life. He wants to "give lessons in feeling" that will shatter complacency, and he develops his own brand of realistic dramaturgy to accomplish this goal. *Look Back in Anger* contributed nothing to the advancement of dramatic technique. If we want, therefore, to understand its reception as an epoch-making play, we must look at the main currents in social and theatrical history at the moment of *Anger*'s appearance.

Since Gladstone's ministry in the 1880s, changes in British history have traced a bifurcated curve: along one line the shrinking of empire, along the other a continuation of the gradual incursions of domestic reform that began just before Victoria's ascension. Both movements have been bitterly resisted by an entrenched ruling class and encouraged by a spectrum of liberal activist factions. Two world wars temporarily interrupted these social and political processes, but the two international holocausts were sandwiched between irreversible internal upheavals: the Boer and Irish risings, Palestine, and Gandhi's thirty years of resistance. In 1945, the Labour party won an impressive victory, a mandate for the welfare state and the breakdown of the class system. After an unavoidable period of postwar austerity, an era of affluence was predicted, and a meritocracy that would supersede the reign of the old school tie. But empire doesn't die painlessly, nor privilege gracefully phase itself out, nor liberalism wield power without compromise. The welfare state became an actuality, but price control and socialized medicine were no magical panaceas. As one of the popular clichés of the early fifties put it: "Nobody is very well and the state of the fare is rotten." By 1951, it was apparent that the great come-and-get-it day hadn't dawned, so Clement Attlee was voted out and Winston Churchill in and it was obvious that England, like all democracies, was to endure alternating eras of reaction and reform. And the egalitarian common man, perhaps a fantasy figure of the socialist intellectuals, instead of overthrowing dead symbols that retarded his liberty, was lining up by the millions for Elizabeth II's coronation. Many dreams were squashed as that common man declared himself willing to settle for "a fridge, a washer, and a telly . . . that's all I want in life."

In light of these serious blows to the self-esteem of the radical sensibility, slight disruptions of the class system, such as the burgeoning of red-brick universities, seemed to redouble rather than ameliorate the frustration of intellectual youth. With England testing H-bombs and approaching the Suez fiasco, that desperate Tory endgame of empire, the time was overripe for a theater of protest. The socialist critic Kenneth Tynan was begging for such a theater: "How is it that political plays aren't being turned out in England at the present time? How is it that we have no tradition of political theater?"

One reason was the control of public theater by state censorship; another was simply that no one was writing powerful anti-Establishment drama. There were harbingers of an emerging mood of angry defiance in the first novels of John Wain and Kingsley Amis. But the British theater had no rebel commanding a wide audience until Osborne's appearance. As Peter Brook noted in reference to the tremendous theatrical breakthrough represented by the arrival of a spokesman for this mood: "The right imagination isn't always there. John Osborne's achievement is that one day he gave form where no one else saw that form lay." Theater, however, is big business, and the gap between writing a serious play and getting a hearing for it can be immense. In addition to a seemingly innocuous censorship that quietly but surely prevented any truly dissentient play from reaching a mass audience, the producers themselves were hemmed in by financial pressure; only plays likely to sell could be put on. The British theater was choking in the stranglehold of politeness and safety. Osborne was lucky, though, for several theater practitioners were chafing against caution and dedicating themselves to building a theater of experiment and chance. Whether it was a happy configuration of circumstances or the inexorable coalescence of an idea whose time had come, the English Stage Company, a private subscription theater not subject to censorship, was being formed by the actor George Devine just as Osborne was writing *Look Back in Anger.* Devine hoped to discover new dramatic talent and to tap the unexplored resources of established writers in other forms. He encouraged novelists like Nigel Dennis to write plays, offering them freedom from the fear of having to tailor their work for the West End. The company advertised for plays, received Osborne's in the mail, and opened *Anger* as its third production at the Royal Court, thereby changing the geography of postwar British theater.

After a segment of the play was shown on TV, it became a sellout hit. The West End smelled sweet success in the marketing of protest and a double front—the commercial theater in addition to the English Stage Company—was opened for the young "engaged" playwright who could suddenly hope to have more than his wife for an audience. *Anger's* subject matter and dissenting point of view proved a watershed for a flood of regional and working-class plays, most of them realistic. An intensely hostile public quickly reacted against the "new drama," but a sympathetic, loyal audience also evolved to support it. The British theater leaped into a life it has not yet lost, although the initial excitement of a new movement has long faded.

Look Back in Anger is by no means the first play reviewers mistook it for. During his years on the provincial stage Osborne wrote several unpublished plays. Sketchy summaries survive of two which were performed out of London: *The Devil Inside Him* (written with Stella Linden, 1950; revived in 1962 as *Cry for Love* by "Robert Owen") and *Personal Enemy. Anger* was written in what became Osborne's customary manner—a long contemplative stage followed by swift composition (nine days) with next to no revision. Its construction betrays haste; an old-fashioned, one-set realistic play, it is a textbook case of the dangers inherent in peepholism. There are announcements of arrivals, timely entrances to delay revelation of crucial information, and woefully inelegant stretches of exposition (e.g., a husband explains to his wife the sources of the financing for his business after they've been married three years). There are even a few gooey snatches of dialogue, such as: "I've always wanted you—always!" or "I've never seen such hatred in someone's eyes before. It's slightly horrifying. Horrifying and oddly exciting." And the basic plot devices are ancient: misalliance compounded by a triangle. Yet, so stageworthy is the play that these weaknesses go unnoticed in the rush of performance. If it seems at too many moments that we've tuned in on "Peyton Place," we must simply acknowledge the faults and pass on. Otherwise we risk losing the immense passion and excitement of a play not mired in trivial melodramatics but concerned with presenting a world to which chaos has come.

In the early fifties, the psychoanalyst Allen Wheelis wrote about a profound change in the nature of emotional distress.

Wheelis's description is helpful in understanding Osborne's central characters from both psychological and historical perspectives. Earlier in this century, according to Wheelis, psychoanalytic treatment had greater clarity than today. A patient was perhaps a hysteric suffering from a traumatic sexual repression; dig deeply enough and cure was likely. But now, Wheelis poignantly goes on, the person who comes for help is usually suffering from constant anxiety, sexual inadequacies and fears, lifelong loneliness, and a persistent sense of helplessness and meaninglessness. How, Wheelis asks, can a psychoanalyst's skill cure the modern condition? In *Look Back in Anger,* Osborne's ferocious embodiment of this condition is Jimmy Porter. Jimmy is a caged animal, the shell of the fine and aspiring human being he was before he stopped hoping and began to fester. We encounter him late in his progressive disintegration. He is frozen into compulsive repetition of attack on the political Establishment and on his loved ones, and this is his only way to unleash the tension of enormous unchanneled energy.

Jimmy dominates the play, a figure of commanding psychological interest. He spills his boundless fury on everything either in sight or dredged up from an astounding data bank of antipathies. His behavior is morbidly cruel and self-contradictory. Terrified of abandonment, Jimmy is determined to prove that the world is unloving as he imagines it to be, and he systematically lashes at all who care for him. His anxiety-plagued life is a self-fulfilling prophecy of betrayal and loss, of impotent insight that produces no change. Jimmy functions according to what has been called the "neurotic's 100% principle": he exacts *total* allegiance, *impossible* tokens of love and commitment, *utter* sensitivity which precludes the needs of others. Needless to say, Jimmy's narcissism, paranoia, sado-masochism, and escapist nostalgia for maternalism and the womb have been fully noted by those who find the manifest political content of his "malad-

[8]

justment" upsetting and who respond by discounting him as a self-pitying child unable to test or face reality.

Undeniably, Osborne irritated a bundle of exposed nerves in the body politic. It is impossible to be indifferent to Jimmy; one either defensively dismisses him or confronts the political implications of his protest and the social etiology of his anguish. Like his personality, Jimmy's dissent too has been labeled adolescent and neurotic, usually by "normals" (as Archie Rice of *The Entertainer* calls them) who are precisely the architects of the social structure that Jimmy despises. Most marvelous in the barrage of responses intended to neutralize the sting of Osborne's venom was the London *Times* critic's summing up of Jimmy: "a thoroughly cross young man." Terence Rattigan, master of the Shaftesbury Avenue long run and symbol to the young dramatists of everything wrong with the British theater, took *Anger* personally, condemning Osborne's sole purpose as "Look, Ma, how unlike Terence Rattigan I'm being." And there is Somerset Maugham's famous blanket dismissal of all the working-class intellectuals of the fifties: "They are scum!" Osborne had clearly taken on a formidable enemy, the power elite which is able to smother with politely bored miscomprehension.

Osborne's audience could only have been the frustrated left. Eric Bentley has reminded us that disaffiliated theater is by definition addressed to the disaffiliated. And this includes especially the young. As Kenneth Tynan said in his famous review of the play, the disquiet of those seven millions in Britain between twenty and thirty was expressed in Jimmy's frustration. For *Look Back in Anger* gave a generation a measure of itself. It articulated the rampant, undirected anger against a cynical political structure so bent on self-perpetuation and so successful at it that all idealistic aspiration seemed pointless. It dispelled, too, any illusion that the pursuit of happiness in personal relationships could remain independent of social reality. As Bernard

Beckerman has written, paying *Look Back in Anger* high tribute, it "aroused people to reinterpret their lives in terms defined by the theater."

While Osborne is hypercritical of Jimmy's destructiveness, he is profoundly aware of the external causes of Jimmy's rancor, full of compassion for his fate, and wholly in agreement with the social protest themes of Jimmy's invective. Jimmy operates within an ironclad value system, an absolutely clear-cut division of good and evil. Evil is the Establishment with its icons of success and adjustment, its complacent blandness. There is Alison's off-stage brother Nigel, backbone of the empire, an ambitious Tory M.P. who couldn't smell suffering if his aristrocratic nose were smeared with it. And there is the Church—which, together with the monarchy and the media, forms Osborne's obsessive triumvirate of bêtes noires—finely symbolized by the bells pounding in the claustrophobic attic set, the Church that would crumble if ever it had to confront a genuine human need in the here and now. A little Sunday going-to-meeting evades the pain of being alive, sidesteps the grappling with reality without which there can be no glimmer of redemption, no dream of grace. So Jimmy quotes the newspapers on the Anglican bishop who wants everyone to pitch in to "assist in the manufacture of the H-bomb" or recounts (with a humor that reveals vestiges of the charm and energy that won him the cloistered Alison) the story of the lady who was stampeded as she stood up for Christ at a Billy Graham revival. Revival is the word—Jimmy stands for life again, here and now. The bells which are pulling Alison away, her father's nostalgia for colonial days, and the Sandhurst morals of Nigel all stand for death-in-life. Against the self-confident, zombie world rung in by the stately bells Jimmy opposes the jazz wail of his trumpet. The disordered, aching sufferer blasts a futile raspberry at the unheeding world. In a society that prizes emotional deadness, Jimmy struggles for openness, spontaneity, and vulnerability. His trumpet is his way of nay-saying—a gesture as moving, proud, and hopeless as Archie Rice's giving a defiant fig to his anonymous, unresponding audience at the end of *The Entertainer.*

Jimmy is the outsider fighting to hold on to a dwindling, all-but-lost sense of inner worth in a society that has engineered the big bomb. This monstrous society not only suffocates the idealist but threatens universal obliteration, with the Nigels at the button. To Jimmy's generation the H-bomb, which hadn't yet been psychologically rationalized by mutual deterrence or long ladders of escalation or hot lines, stood as an absolute index of the failure of men to live as brothers. Jimmy's frenzy is like a sustained anxiety attack, a deeply sunk fear of meaninglessness. In the tense rhythms of his tirades he expresses our pervasive contemporary anxiety and the flailing, objectless violence that is both relief from and an exact measure of our terror. "If the big bang does come, and we all get killed off, it won't be in aid of the old-fashioned grand design. . . . About as pointless and inglorious as stepping in front of a bus."

Look Back in Anger, then, is more than a play of social protest. It is a virtual compendium of urgent mid-century concerns: isolation and alienation, noncommunication, the death of ideals and the vanishing of heroism, identity crisis and the disintegration of the self, the struggle for authenticity within the technological explosion, the confrontation of nothingness, the uselessness of awareness for changing a cruel world. Unlike Pinter or Beckett, Osborne is not concerned with incorporating his themes into timeless-seeming mythic patterns but prefers a traditional domestic form in which idea inheres in relationships and conflicts. He is willing to sacrifice density of poetic texture in favor of a hyperactive whirlwind rhetoric that mirrors not a cosmic condition but the frantic second-to-second living of pain-filled lives, "the very narrow strip of plain hell" we inhabit.

Thought, then, must be abstracted from a play which is essentially a piece of psychological realism arranged to bring to critical points the lives of four particular people "responding nakedly to the burden of trying to live" inside the absurdity of unchanging boredom, a despondent eternal sameness beautifully symbolized by the triple repetition of the reading of the Sunday papers and by the precise replacement of wife Alison by mistress Helena at the ironing board. All four have choices to make; three decide to clear out. Although the world of the play may occasionally seem like Beckett's game of chess in which the object is to move all the pieces out and back without losing a man, the loss at the end is real. Jimmy is abandoned by all who love him. He is like an addict who requires ever larger doses of others' hurt to escape his own, until the supply is exhausted. Alison's miscarriage and condemnation to lifelong barrenness is the overdose that makes Jimmy realize he has truly been killing himself — a mushily sentimental denouement. No one could ever accuse Osborne of being a master plotter; in almost every play there are flagrant instances of faulty story-line manipulations of emotion. But Alison's return and the movement toward reconciliation hardly provide a true-love-conquers-all final curtain. The play ends with a needy embrace as they hold onto each other knowing they are forever alone in a hostile world. Only by consciously accepting a life-lie, by nurturing the fantasy of comfort and by playing at love, can they go on, with no guarantee of freedom from further pain. There is no tragedy but no triumph either. Just four people trying to live, learning that "men live and they are not happy."

Perhaps the most damning charge leveled at the play is that it has dated: it was the right play in the right place at the right time, but it has lost its sting in a rapidly changing world where the conditions of its origin no longer hold true. My own sense is that *Anger* will continue to be meaningful as long as we can conceive of a finer world; that it will have heightened point at moments when a significant segment of a society feels disenfranchised. Surely, with its laceratingly ironic vision of idealism jolt-

[12]

ed into the tragic sense of life, it is a play for America today, an America that has been losing its vaunted innocence with increasing agony since the first Kennedy assassination. *Anger*'s real limit, I think, shows up in the ending. It is a *young* play and suffers from a circumscribed emotional range as it probes rather shrilly but with lazerlike penetration into early sorrow and the ugly fact that the world never lives up to youthful expectation. I often assign the play to my students (mostly urbanites in their twenties) who find that it has power and immediacy as an accurate portrait of basic problems they are struggling with. Osborne himself, forty, famous, rich, and married four times, says the play "embarrasses" him now. It shouldn't; it still has abundant life.

Epitaph for George Dillon (1958), written with Anthony Creighton, presents minor problems in chronology. The earliest of Osborne's surviving plays, it was the third produced. A rigorous treatment by order of composition makes sense; *Epitaph* is vastly inferior to *Anger* in every way: plot, thought, feeling, characterization, style, and theatricality. Placing *Epitaph* first allows a gratifying demonstration of an amazing leap in Osborne's art, but violates *theatrical* history in the extraordinary case of so historically important a play as *Look Back in Anger*. Yet to deal with the plays as the world came to know them would force *Epitaph* into position after *The Entertainer*, where it would dangle in space as evidence of the rapid dementia of its author's gifts. There is no compelling case for putting it second, except that it fits there least clumsily, and it has to go somewhere.

In *Epitaph*, Osborne and Creighton take the germ of a promising dramatic idea—the planting of a mediocre artist into the weed patch of petit-bourgeois suburbia—and spoil most of it by hideous plotting and amateurish dialogue that are symptomatic of their insecure grasp of their theme. A bald summary of the story leads one to expect that the authors must have been working tongue in cheek, but there is no way to get around the fact that the plot is awful. George Dillon is an unsuccessful thirty-three-year-old minitalented actor and would-be dramatist endowed with enough egoism for several stars. He is too fragile for the workaday world, so he manages to maneuver himself into permanent parasitism in the lower middle-class Elliot household. Mrs. Elliot just happens to be searching for a surrogate son to replace her Raymond, a war casualty. George soon approaches a *Beggar on Horseback* crisis: whether to keep believing in his untested art or to sell out and stay in the Elliot womb, a helpless spiritual cripple but a solid success as smut peddler to the provinces. In the course of the most contrived and jejune last act in recent memory, George contracts and recovers from TB; impregnates the youngest Elliot; confesses a nondissolved marriage; and makes a bundle from his play "Telephone Tart," which is put on by a producer who has walked in the Elliot front door unsummoned. Unsurprisingly, George winds up as one of the Elliots, calling Mrs. Elliot "Mum" in the curtain line.

Yet the play is not instantly dismissible. Within this atrocious scaffolding it does manage to convey some dramatic fire and thematic suggestiveness. The first act is an obvious but effective satiric evocation of the tension and meanness of the representative Elliot domicile. Mrs. Elliot is an able caricature of the typical matriarch of aspidistra-land. "Emotionally restrained," spelling out S-E-X and recoiling at "damn," she rules relentlessly with her demolishing well-meaningness. The act explores the spiritual wasteland of middle-class hypocritical respectability (that keynote on which modern drama began): look the other way when your daughter goes upstairs to get in the family way if it'll land her a "suitable" husband; drown the loneliness and lack of meaningful communication in a nice cup of tea and orgies of telly; measure inner worth by material success, which automatically entitles the bearer not only to forgiveness but to obeisance.

Osborne and Creighton never see virtue, as Orwell did, in the stubborn endurance of the basic unit of the British social structure.

The burden of the play, however, falls on the progressive failure and isolation of George. Like the other protagonists of Osborne's early plays, Dillon is the self-appointed center of awareness and sincerity withering among "these people" whose "existence is one great cliché." George is one of what Eugene O'Neill called the fog people, one of William James's "sick souls" who never feel at home in life, cursed by a morbid self-consciousness that never lets them merge with the flux of things. The authors avoid the sentimental or tragic possibilities that Osborne stresses in both *Look Back in Anger* and *The Entertainer.* George is treated ironically, deserving the fate he vilifies. He is essentially a coward, unwilling to take chances, an Elliot before he knows it. The point is brought uncomfortably home that most of us are little people who make the craven choice in hundreds of little ways. Yet we are never convinced that Dillon's capitulation is in any way a pity or a waste.

But there are stretches, and these are the fire of the play, when George does matter. In the electric confrontation between George and Ruth (a rebel Elliot, educated, leftist, nonvirginal, and worldly wise), George is the prototypical modern intellectual hemmed in by self-doubt and despondency. He touches Ruth and us. To protect himself from the naked truth of self, George has been acting the cynical, detached role so long that only extremes of shame, desire, or self-disgust demarcate any longer where his "brilliant" routines end and *he* begins. And the tiny territory of self-respect is shrinking rapidly. He has some vestige of self-value which enables him to reach out briefly to Ruth, but he is beyond reclamation. The sexual tension of the scene is remarkable, every bit as powerful as that in the second act of *Anger,* where intense sexuality is manifested as verbal aggression. Failing with Ruth, hating himself, George turns in

[15]

cold fury and violence to Josie and the pretense of escape in detached animal lust.

Osborne is superb in his dramatizations of the psychological configurations of modern sexuality. Sex is a cardinal Osborne subject, primarily as symptom and expression of anxiety. It is entirely absent from only one of his sixteen plays, and is prominently placed in the foreground of nine. In *Anger,* sex was another item in Jimmy Porter's inexhaustible list of disappointments; Alison just wasn't the Real McCoy of every Portnoy's fantasies. Too, there were undercurrents in Jimmy of passivity and dependence, anxious fears of cannibalistic devouring of his genitals in coitus, but Osborne never did anything with these disturbing nuances. In *Epitaph,* sex is more concretely dramatized as a "shabby" expense of spirit, another step in the process of self-loss, an ineffective reassurance that because we touch another body we exist ourselves. The momentary spilling of tenseness only magnifies the post-coital tristfulness, providing another piece of evidence of lovelessness and the horror of absolute nonconnectedness. Among postwar playwrights, no one surpasses Osborne in delineating the humiliating sexual aspect of unhappiness. There is, then, some very serious thinking tucked amidst the over-all ineptitude of the play. Nevertheless, *Epitaph* remains undeniably only very promising prentice work.

The Entertainer (1957) is the most controlled and balanced of Osborne's early plays. Like *Look Back in Anger* it is a protest play, and like *Epitaph for George Dillon,* a play about an ungifted actor coping with personal and professional failure. Lacking the flamboyant verbal audacity of the former, and to its credit, the flat unrelieved defeatist landscape of the latter, *The Entertainer* gathers many of the concerns of both into a more muted and measured pattern, one rich in structural intricacy, emotional variety, and metaphysical overtone.

In a form illustrating Osborne's growing dissatisfaction with "the restrictions of the realistic stage," *The Entertainer* tells the story of six members of the Rice family during and shortly after the Suez crisis. Closed-in "at-home" scenes alternate in ironic counterpoint with Archie Rice's sleazy burlesque numbers. Music hall rotted into a nudie show, Archie's variety turns grotesquely transmogrify the everyday anguish of the realistic family scenes into a resonant image of universal angst. The two distinct tones are unified by the dominant presence of Archie. They are also linked by Osborne's ubiquitous political judgment of England, a colonial power in the same terminal stage of decay as Archie's music hall. The Suez crisis surrounds and points the action of the play as Osborne skillfully welds the historic to the domestic. As in *Look Back in Anger,* it is impossible in *The Entertainer* to consider private suffering apart from politics. The play fixes the grim humor of Archie's long-standing desperation and the sharp pain of his children's disillusion within an imperial England still using gunboat diplomacy in the atomic age. *The Entertainer* is *Heartbreak House* forty years later—heartbroken house.

The three generations of Rices incorporate three clashing world views as Osborne interweaves politics and private destinies. Archie's father, Billy, was a headliner at the tag end of the music hall era around World War I. He is the perfect model of vestigial Edwardianism: on the positive side he has all the arrogant self-confidence stemming from the possession of an unquestioned place in a predictable world order. Along with his secure identity he also has all the vicious prejudices—racist, jingoist, puritanical—that go with his self-righteous morality, a morality as inadequate in the modern world as the colonial policies of the government. Most like him is his grandson Mick, who knows his duty and loves his country, or at any rate follows orders. We don't meet him; he is a "national hero" off being slaughtered at Suez, for in Osborne's world there is irony and pity, but no reward for idealism on the right or left. And Billy himself never suspects that his values have anything to do with

Mick's death, that *his* government sent Mick to Suez. Like the father in Hebbel's *Maria Magdalena*, he doesn't understand the world anymore. He can complain about it or scorn it (he does both nonstop), but he is blind to his generation's responsibility for it.

Osborne has been accused, too hastily I think, of a severe romantic nostalgia for Edwardian simplicities and a solid, golden world long gone. This view assumes Jimmy Porter is his spokesman: "If you've no world of your own it's rather pleasant to regret the passing of someone else's." More precisely, nostalgia functions in Osborne's plays as one of those too-small escape hatches in which we get stuck and then are forced to climb back down to consciousness of unsalvable distress. Everyone, faced with the giant dilemmas of living in the unpleasant now (like Archie's income tax man waiting in the wings, or Jean Rice's inability to shut her eyes to the degradation and injustice around her), longs for a little peace and relief. We shape ineffective symbols, fantasy barbiturates to quiet the racing brain. They don't work; we know we are playing a losing game against reality. Archie's detached routines, his sex and liquor, Jimmy Porter's rants and the pervasive looking back are similar strategies to ward off the demons of awareness. In Osborne's plays nostalgia is never automatically a positive value like caring, openness, vulnerability, or spontaneity. The nostalgic posture always expresses character and inner conflict. Politically, Osborne insists that the heritage of Edwardianism is the inhumanity of present-day power politics. Psychologically, his characters are flayed by inculcated ego ideals of unity and accomplishment they can never live up to. No wonder so much of the looking back is in anger. Who cannot rage at his own fragmentation? Nostalgia, then, is never a serious pitfall in Osborne's thinking. It is an attribute of his characterology.

Billy Rice has, so to speak, killed Mick Rice. But his two other grandchildren, cursed with conscience and sensitivity, are

[18]

no patriots. For them, life has to offer more than an opportunity to "speed down the middle of the road together." Both try to trust their impulse to rebel and seek to build an authentic self-hood resistant to the pressures of the acquisitive society. Frank fails; Jean makes a start. Frank had been a conscientious objector, jailed for his convictions. But in the light of Suez and Mick's death he is convinced his refusal was an empty gesture. For Frank, Sartre is wrong. We are free to say no, but saying no, with all the willingness to take any consequences, doesn't matter a damn. The system's too big and we can't dent it. So Frank gives up, his idealism seared to ashes in a cruel world, and adopts a false mask of cynicism (as one of Archie's songs goes: "We're all out for good Old Number One"). He takes the first step down Archie's road toward an elaborately structured pretense of non-engagement. Whatever his future, it is clear that Frank's bitter departure is part of the unarrestable process of waste that corrodes England. Britain is losing the best of her sons. The patriots are slaughtered, the idealists are broken. It is the Grahams (Jean's fiancé) with "the decent little careers lined up" who stay and, no harm meant, begin the march to the next Suez.

Jean Rice is the most attractive personality of the play. Tender, generous, she is what Archie calls a sentimentalist: "you carry all your responses about with you, instead of leaving them at home"—a fatal weakness in an achieving society but one that immediately marks her as a highly valenced carrier of values in Osborne's world. The play catches her at a critical moment when a whole former system of values suddenly seems overwhelmingly false. She is rootless and has come home again to try to anchor herself briefly and find her way. As she lives through the deaths of her brother and grandfather, her stepmother's hysterical time-serving in the prison of a dreary life, and her father's shoulder-shrugging detachment, she experiences a clear awakening to the tragic reality of life: "Here we are, we're alone in the universe, there's no God, it all began by something as simple as sunlight striking on a piece of rock. And here we are. We've only got ourselves. Somehow, we've just got to make a go of it." This may sound like anthology-culled existentialism, but it is really a true cry in the wilderness, deeply felt philosophy. In its bleak resignation lies the birth of affirmation, for we are lonely but not alone. What remains for Jean is to ask the question at the center of the play: knowing the odds against happiness, facing raw reality, how are we to live? Like Osborne himself, she emerges with boundless sympathy. Her astonishment at injustice is intact, and she will reach out to her fellow sufferers as best she can, failing probably, but with dignity. She refuses to crawl inside the whale Archie-style and "let it pass over me." She says "no" to conforming Graham and to Archie's depressive warning that she'll end up "just as dead and smug and used up, and sitting on your hands like everybody else." Maybe she will, but she won't quit in advance. Perhaps all we can do is make useless gestures in the void. But what has utility to do with man's search for a way to love?

Jean's crisis is important, yet it is Archie Rice who is the title character and whose destiny forms the play's final image. Like Jimmy Porter and Bill Maitland (in *Inadmissible Evidence*) Archie is a favorite Osborne character: the bastard we can't help caring about. Archie is played out in every way: he never had much talent; his show is closing and the income tax man (read: Death) is waiting in the wings; his family has dissolved; he has emotional gangrene and is conscienceless; his shoddy sexual adventures aren't the ego-builders and painkillers they used to be. He can no longer distinguish between defiantly working a hostile audience and playing the hack comedian at home, where he simply has nothing to give. Archie is bright, articulate, and lost, but carrying on with gritty endurance. Osborne means him as an image of the human situation: he *inhabits* that void Jean has looked out at. Osborne is particularly fascinated by people who have the capacity for great suffering and the imagination to grasp the universal validity of their experience but lack the artistic or intellectual genius to give their feelings form. An armless man trying to reach out eventually grasps the comedy of his falling down every time. So he learns either to stop reaching or to be deliberately ludicrous, playing his mutilation for all it's worth. But once in a while, in the pride of keeping going until the bitter end (Archie refuses a profitable 9-to-5 job in Canada: he is going to die *his* way), or in that moment at the end of Act II when he keens a blues over Mick's death, Archie is magnificently human, tragic, and suffering for all of us. Like the man in his last joke (his jokes have a way of turning into parables) who curses in paradise to the immense relief of the Heavenly Hosts, Archie is the subversive who annihilates righteous humbug. When he leaves the stage at play's end, it is "bare and dark." And we, the audience he has been working all along, realize how valuable he is only as we lose him. For in his presence we don't have to play at being better than we are, or pretend that everything is just lovely, thank you.

We ultimately judge a play by the extent to which it calls into action the complex responses we are capable of, by how deeply alive it makes us feel. Though it lacks the driving passion of *Inadmissible Evidence*'s total absorption in one man's life and though it has a third act which suffers from Osborne's congenital inability to let enough plot alone, *The Entertainer* remains the most broadly gratifying of his plays, the one that actuates the widest range of our sympathies.

The Entertainer concludes the first phase of Osborne's career. All three plays belonging to this period are primarily realistic, deal with invented (as opposed to historical) characters, and center upon the tribulations of a hypersensitive, defensive, defeated male protagonist in a family setting. We might label it his "socialist" phase, for the plays all fulfill Osborne's descrip-

[21]

tion of his "socialist attitude" at the time they were written:

Socialism is an experimental idea, not a dogma; an attitude to truth and liberty, the way people live and treat each other . . . an experimental attitude to feeling. . . . Nobody can be very interested in my contribution to a problem like the kind of houses people should have built for them. . . . But there are other questions to be asked—how do people live inside those houses? What is their relationship with one another? . . . What are the things that . . . make them care, give them hope and anxiety? What are their expectations? What moves them, brings them together, makes them speak out? Where is the weakness, the loneliness? . . . Where is the strength? . . . these are the questions of socialism.

Osborne doesn't abandon socialism at this point; his criticism of England is always launched from left of the Labour party. But it is in the first three plays that he addresses himself most directly and repeatedly to the "questions of socialism" with a severe truthfulness to the way we live now. They form the first and last coherent *group* of his plays. After *The Entertainer* his work takes three tacks on no consistent developmental course: social satire; historical reinterpretation; and intermittent returns to his earliest interest, the revelation of individual personality within family relationships and a contemporary environment.

Discussion of Osborne's work since 1958 must begin with a dismaying fact that cannot be glossed over: he has written several unredeemably bad plays. They are sandwiched in between excellent work, with such regularity that the composition of a couple of complete fiascos almost seems prerequisite for his imagination to yield up a play of substance.

If *The World of Paul Slickey* (1959), a catch-all satirical musical comedy, were Osborne's first play it would never have survived the discard pile of some producer's unsolicited manuscripts. The most salient fact about the play is its survival, for any writer with a shred of self-criticism would have scrapped it. But not only did Osborne direct it himself and bring it into a big London theater, he felt compelled to counterattack violently the near-unanimous critical onslaught. Although the play was overpraised in some quarters for its brash frankness, *Slickey's* sophomoric execution denies it the significance it was hastily assigned as a breakthrough of the musical comedy genre into ideological seriousness. *Slickey* does allow Osborne to strike at dozens of his best-loved antagonisms. Within the framework of a silly farcical story about a noble family which is trying to keep its daddy alive for forty-eight hours to beat the inheritance tax, Osborne manages to attack drama criticism, stage censorship, advertising, the effete peerage, the church, indiscriminate sexuality, pop culture, and above all the invasion of privacy in the press's abuse of its limitless power. There's no doubt John Osborne is a man who knows what he doesn't like. But after enduring the "organized triviality" of *Slickey* (Osborne uses the phrase in the play to describe England), one can only paraphrase Alceste's advice to Oronte: When the urge to write this kind of stuff comes over you, control it.

In *A Subject of Scandal and Concern* (1960), his first TV play and the first of his three history plays, Osborne tries to regain control. He revives the forgotten story of George Holyoake, who in 1842 was the victim of a Victorian witch-hunt and the last person in England imprisoned for blasphemy. The play in itself is small beer compared to the theatrical richness of other work, but it marks a return to competence (no more than that yet) after the babbling of *Slickey*. Of all Osborne's plays, it is the most conventional and clear-cut in conflict and theme, the simplest in technique. Holyoake, a little-league version of Ibsen's Brand, sacrifices family ties to put his Owenite principles into practice. He is an isolated moral absolutist (that is, an Osborne rebel-idealist on the side of the angels) who calls down upon himself the big battalions of a wealthy church and an entrenched legal system. By means of an uninspired trial scene no different from a thousand others, Osborne provides himself with yet another opportunity to parade some of his familiar indictments against the British system. In the forefront is the truism that

[23]

institutions seek to perpetuate themselves and destroy some individuals in the process. This elementary fact of political nature continually strikes Osborne with the force of idealism's first fall from innocence, and he is always able to poke his shocked indignation into renewed flame without resorting to the tedious cliché bludgeons of agitprop.

In this little play, however, Osborne's analysis of society's dynamics cuts deeper than before. In the course of Holyoake's self-defense, Osborne explicitly introduces a strand of thought latent in previous plays. Power in a democracy depends upon a symbiotic relationship between the governors and the governed. Men are ruled by their consent, and slowly, by a kind of psychic suicide, they die imaginatively and ultimately emotionally because they allow themselves to worship the slogans and symbols of self-interested power groups. Real change begins with individual awareness of unfreedom. Osborne's theater demands that we examine the destructiveness of the isms we live by: patriotism, materialism, republicanism, don't rock the boatism, even institutionalized socialism. His assumption, shrieking out from every scene in *The Entertainer* and *Look Back in Anger,* is that our culture has had it, and we'd better start reevaluating our priorities or go down with that unrocked boat. This is why Holyoake's story, in itself a trivial one (he only served six months), is to Osborne a subject of concern which demands that we confront its implications. How are we maintaining oppressive structures in the guise of cherished ideals? What can still happen to the man of principle if he speaks out and his principles are dangerous to the status quo? How much time do we have in the hydrogen age to discover that we are cut off from community, so concerned with respectability and success that we no longer know what dignity and liberty are?

The play raises these touchy issues, but unfortunately they bob on its surface unanchored to a substantial dramatic action. Osborne never masters the history play as a vehicle for posing the questions that might begin a reexamination of worn-out values. No present-day dramatist has, despite the recent popularity of the form. But in his next play, *Luther* (1961), Osborne writes as interesting a failure as any.

By the end of the fifties, the imprint of Brecht had been indelibly stamped on the British theater. George Devine had returned from a 1956 visit with Brecht to stage *The Good Woman of Setzuan,* which followed *Look Back in Anger* into the Royal Court. The Berliner Ensemble also played a London season in 1956, and in the late fifties and sixties Brecht-like chronicle plays seemed to flow as plentifully as Archie Rice's beloved draught Bass. The interruptions and jarring discontinuity of the Brechtian history play perfectly mirror the existentialist contention that we inhabit a contiguous, not a continuous, universe. The flexible Brechtian style lends itself readily to high philosophical seriousness, but far more often it deteriorated into mere stagey storytelling, substanceless pageantry cashing in on Brecht's discoveries. Popular too was (and still is) the Brechtian fallible hero of the Galileo variety, the genius who is an inextricable compound of intellect, humanity, irony, and bodily self-involvement. Ever since Büchner's Danton, the man who dons the heroic mask of rebellion without letting us forget the fleshy face underneath, we have preferred great men (in plays, at least) to have sexual organs, stomachs, addictions, vanity. We like our Falstaffs and Henry V's rolled into one, and we respond in almost automatic agreement to the ironic deflation of puristic ideals. As Danton says, every step forward is taken over a corpse; the modern sensibility finds any other view of history sentimental. Consequently, today's history play must either offer a sardonic perspective on history or rest content to be entertainment or propaganda.

With Brechtism so much in the air, Osborne sooner or later had to write a multiscene history play with a dominating, ironically treated protagonist. After discontent with fourth-wall realism led him to the originality of the counterpoint structure of *The Entertainer* and then, in *The World of Paul Slickey*, to an inept extreme of stylized artifice, Osborne finally found in the history play a way to swing back to some kind of formal balance between the public and private spheres. The history play is potentially the ideal form for uniting, within a freer use of open theater, his rhetorical excellence, social criticism, and his absorption in the moral and psychological crises of a dynamic central figure.

Supreme rebel against the global Establishment, Luther seems an inexorable Osborne choice. The play was conceived when Osborne came upon Erik H. Erikson's landmark contribution to psychobiography, *Young Man Luther*, a study that shares the theater's tendency to de-heroicize genius. Erikson (Osborne's sole biographical source) provides an interpretation of the link between Luther's outer achievement and his physical obsessiveness and exacerbated father fixation. Sonhood is the psychological pivot on which both book and play revolve. Like Hamlet, Osborne's Luther is too much in the son, immersed in an identity crisis generated by his filial position. The play opens with a willed isolation from community as Luther's profession of monastic life demands repudiation of his earthly father (an apostle of worldly success) in favor of a heavenly one and the yoke of obedience imposed by His terrestrial surrogate, the infallible pope. The spine of the play consists of a zestful psychological treatment of Luther's ambivalence in this role. He alternates violently between submissive obedience and mockery via an overexact practice of the strict letter of monastic regimen. He must be less than nothing, a worm, or a colossal egoist, the vilest of sinners. One moment he denies his conception by any father, the next he insists on being the perfect son to an all-demanding Father: an inner conflict of rich dramatic proportions.

Luther's revolutionary theological precept—justification by faith alone—is a consequence of working through (but never wholly resolving) his sonship. Osborne shows us a Luther deriving his own brand of existentialism on the rack of bodily and spiritual suffering. Since we can never, by any behavior or ploys on our part, be certain that we please our fathers, nor by any strategy indemnify a father's love, we live with an ultimate insecurity as the essence of being: "there's no security, there's no security at all, either in indulgences, holy busywork or anywhere in this world." Radical doubt about the father's requitement of the son's infinite love and yearning for consolation can lead, in a figure so absolutely demanding of himself and others and so intellectually endowed, to melancholia or to a formulation that changes the world. Osborne builds terrific tension out of the texture of Luther's extraordinary despair, primarily by massive quotation of Luther's own racy prose. Several images and activities heighten the intensity of anguish: a contorted naked man tied to a sword dangling over the void; the recurrent impaction of Luther's bowels; the lost child symbolizing the "utter abandonment" that is the source of despair.

Osborne's challenge is to give dramatic substance to a Luther in the midst, as Erikson says, of "radically transferring the desperation of his filial position into the human condition vis-à-vis God." The theological result of Luther's agony, a new concept of faith based on identification with the sonhood of the forsaken Christ, doesn't much interest Osborne; the world has been living and debating it for centuries. It is with Luther's personal resolution that he chooses to end the play. A son who can never be sure he pleases his father (nor unconsciously stop trying to please), Luther negotiates an uneasy separate peace by reentering the natural rhythm of ordinary life and, by way of partial reconciliation, fathers a son of his own. Osborne's Luther is, finally, an intellectual giant but no saint or martyr. As his father knew all too well and his wife reminds him: "You like your food, so don't make out you don't." By returning to the human community, Luther comes to a bearable compromise with this world.

[27]

There is no contradiction or belittlement in Osborne's final picture of Luther as paterfamilias, theologically still beset by conflicting rhythms of complete skepticism and tenuous hope, his bowels still knotted, yet able to embrace his son tenderly.

There is more to history than case history. Osborne manages the mass and sweep of the public ceremonial scenes with unexpected facility, but in moving Luther onto the stage of the world he fails to inspire his conflicts with the same surge of conviction informing the private scenes. Sermons, rituals, trial scenes are handled with forensic and dramaturgic adroitness but leave an after-impression of decoration. Clearly Osborne has great temperamental affinity for Luther the man, but as a play of ideas *Luther* disintegrates. The power structure ranged against Luther is made up of the same old strawmen Osborne has been satirizing since Brother Nigel. In this play, the antagonists may be sketched with more assured draftsmanship, but they are inadequate opponents if we are meant to believe Luther's conflict with the Church is as perilous as his psychological conflict. The main problem with *Luther* is that it lacks the kind of sharp clarity of conception that we find in a play of much narrower historical range, such as John Arden's *Sergeant Musgrave's Dance*. Take as evidence the scene in which a knight accuses Martin of carnage in the service of faith and of doublecrossing the peasants who heeded his word. The scene introduces vital new information and the potential for a dialectic of ideal and real, of purpose and consequence, but Osborne does nothing with it, a failure rooted in the dramatist's vacillation between historical authenticity and depth psychology. At their best, his scenes play off each other in an ironic counterpoint of style and theme (Luther's inflexible purity versus Tetzel's hucksterism) but, as in the Peasant Revolt and the closing domestic scenes, too often these self-contained structural units float in the middle of nowhere, like the man on the sword. The only over-all consistency is chronology, and even the sequence of events is confusing once

Osborne gets Luther out of the jakes and into the university. Powerful characterization and language are marred by a form which is like a superb long-distance runner somehow immobilized at the starting line: all taut ligament and tensed muscle —beautiful but not going anywhere.

The most charitable act one could perform for Osborne's next effort, two short plays produced together as *Plays for England* (1962), would be to refrain from exhuming them. Both are smoothly written, avoiding the stylistic atrocities that sunk *The World of Paul Slickey*, but they are as fatally flawed in structure as they are pathetically adolescent in intent. Like Mrs. Elliot, who wanted everything "nice," it would be nice if Osborne hadn't written these and nicer if I didn't have to labor to comment on them. In *Plays for England* the catch-all anger of *Slickey* is narrowed to two prime targets, royalty and the press, but the limited warfare doesn't improve Osborne's satiric aim. His satire is brilliant when it is part of the devastating rants of his gallery of bright, depressive characters, but doubles over when it is made to stand on its own and carry the whole weight of a play.

In the first of these playlets, *The Blood of the Bambergs,* Osborne concocts an irreverent farce in which a photographer covering a royal wedding turns out to be an illegitimate son of the house of Bamberg and is able to pinch-hit when the original bridegroom is killed in a hushed-up collision. (The reference to *the* English royal wedding of the time was obvious.) Osborne uses the farcical plot to lash out at the deceptions of the welfare state (the money spent on royal occasions over a seventeen-year period "could have built . . . twenty-seven secondary schools and 1,200,000 houses"); to abominate the part played by the press in maintaining national respect for the monarchy at the expense of individual liberty (a married lady with three children actually commits suicide onstage over a hopeless passion for the prince); and to expose the betrayals of the politicians who "encourage people to revel in . . . the horseplay of a meaningless symbol. . . . [We] . . . are not conditioned to seriousness but to totem worship." It's the old Osborne chestnut of institutions perpetuating themselves by keeping the masses in the dark. He also takes the opportunity to rejoin battle on the second front opened in *A Subject of Scandal and Concern* against the complicity of the ordinary man in his own oppression. The idolatry of monarchy is an instance of the slave willingly donning his own chains, and monarchy can always be counted upon to provide rituals like the wedding to sustain its hypnotic hold. "Long live our god-like Kings and Queens!" a choir chants at the play's close, as millions cheer in front of TV screens. Osborne wrote this play near the peak of his own political activism, when he was courting arrest to publicize his ban-the-bomb stand, but he fails to create either a dramatic counterpart for his passion or a form to contain his acute analysis of the dangers of "royalty religion." All he can muster is a schoolboy prank.

The second play, *Under Plain Cover,* a diatribe against the press's invasion of privacy, rips in two midway like a pair of too-often patched trousers. Not trousers but knickers are prominent in the first scene, in which an average married couple plays dress-up games to spice their sex life and pass those boring weekends that keep popping up in Osborne's plays. Presumably, Osborne is arguing that what is perverse to society at large is standard operating procedure at home, as if that were news; at any rate, people are to be left alone. For in the second scene the games they had devised for staying reasonably happy are suddenly ended by a reporter's announcement that the couple are brother and sister. The *papparazzi* swarm in to exploit the situation, which has no reason for being in this play (even if it has a factual analogue). The rest of the play is a flailing castigation of the "murderous" disengagement of Fleet Street, which destroys lives to manufacture news. The opening arouses a hopeful expectation that Osborne is picking up on one of his strongest themes, the anatomy of sex in modern life. But we have to wait for his next play for that; in *Under Plain Cover* he leaves us high and dry as he switches midway to an anti-media sermon.

Nothing would have been easier at this lowest point in his creative life than to have written Osborne off as a flash in the pan who had drained his resources in two spectacular years and had been offering up the slag ever since. Then, confounding dire prediction and upholding waning championship, Osborne produced *Inadmissible Evidence* (1964), one of his most impressive "lessons in feeling," a chronicle of the last two days of one man's collapse into forlorn, resigned aloneness. Osborne's power has always been psychological, the revelation of an intensifying anguish over a short period of time. The axis on which his dramatic world (a world of relatively realistic fidelity to observed life) spins is a suffering unto approaching death incorporated in an unpleasant protagonist whose distress is so urgently presented that it strikes us as a metaphysical image of universal import. Although he always deals in extreme cases, Osborne usually presents them within a figurative or representational dramatic structure. He works most comfortably in older, generally discredited, forms. In an age marked by an overridingly negative reaction to realism and a driving pressure on the avant-garde to surpass last week's *ne plus ultra* of abstraction, it is not comfortable to face the fact that one works truest to his talent in an old-fashioned mode. For a few years Osborne floundered outside the mainstream of his imagination's freest play, grappling with and conquering to little purpose the panoramic history play, and going under with satire. At last in *Inadmissible Evidence* he really lets go and writes the monodrama toward which his better plays have always inclined, and fuses his realistic strength with his experimental leanings. By focusing on one character who is going crazy, Osborne is able to move in and out of his protagonist's head, from dream play to realism. Osborne devises an expressive form, incrementally

[31]

decreasing the realistic scenes and increasing the subjective—a form which effectively presents the dynamics of a psychotic break.

The play stands or falls on the degree of representative truth which the spectator grants it: Is Bill Maitland "one of us," a moral paradigm to whom attention must be paid, or just a puling neurotic who cannot get a grip on himself? Does his going to pieces touch deep chords of response and recognition in us, leave us cold, or merely disgust us in its public display of unmanly loss of control and pride? I suspect one either knows in one's bones the cycle of depression and terror, the nagging fear that one's life is a self-tormenting, shameful, guilt-ridden sham, one either knows this as a rock-bottom piece of psychic self-knowing, or one finds the play remote and unsympathetic, frenetic, perhaps curious, but mysterious and apart from one's sense of reality. That is, the play is not universal but special, so true in its delineation of the paranoid depressiveness which is the toll of maladjustment to the acquisitive society that we either find in Maitland a grotesque distorting mirror enlargement of ourselves, taking the play most personally and intimately, or we recoil as from some hideous object we should never have seen. For we are in the territory of the absolute nil, where being is meaningless and an echoing laugh greets our last-ditch proclamation of selfhood: I despair, therefore I am.

Failure ("that is what makes people interesting," Osborne once wrote) and defeat, stark images of impotence, loneliness, and death pervade the play, give it, along with the author's ruthless objectivity, its tone. Shunning his customary heavy-going exposition, Osborne thrusts us into the middle of Maitland's "failure report" in a dream sequence where the thirty-nine-year-old solicitor is on trial before an arbitrary court, like a Strindberg or Kafka or Pinter character, for the very crime of being. Always expecting to be summoned to this accounting, Maitland is caught and squirming between certain guilt and useless self-apology, no more able to conduct his own defense than he can handle any longer his clients' cases. Self-arraigned, guilt-hounded, and unable to make reparation, to redeem the past or begin living better, he wakes from the nightmare to enter his workaday office world where for the rest of the play we watch him *live* his defense and, with the demonic logic of the damned, sabotage his case (in which he is defendant, judge, and jailer) as he moves toward a self-imposed life sentence of isolation. In this most economic of his works, Osborne jettisons everything that would inhibit the spotlighting of Maitland in the now — a self-devouring, gigantic mess of raw need and misery, trying to suck everyone into the quicksand of his despair, clutching greedily for reassurance of the solid reality of his existence, oblivious to anyone's need of him, fully expecting the rejection he invites. Like Jimmy Porter, he engineers the abandonment he most fears, but Maitland, fifteen years older with no reconciliations possible after the fall, has complete insight into the terror of oncoming nothingness and the language to express it: ". . . you're my only grip left, if you'll let me go, I'll disappear, I'll be like something in a capsule in space, weightless, unable to touch anything or do anything, like a groping baby in a removed, putrefied womb."

Crazy? Sure. But Maitland's external profile is frighteningly familiar; like that warped couple in *Who's Afraid of Virginia Woolf?* he is a little too close for comfort too much of the time. His profile reads: married twice, two overprivileged children, suburban home, mistress, frequent casual sexual encounters, struggling to make a go of his own business, bright and verbose, psychosomatic, migraine-prone, potency problems, excessive drinking, insomniac — he could be a commuter on the 5:27. Only he can't pretend anymore. He has lost that little adjustment mechanism for survival that keeps everyone else going and he can no longer kid himself that his work is a humane contribution to a technology-engulfed society he despises, or that the law can make provision for human complexity and suffering, or that his relationships are fulfilling and there's good reason for making that train home. "Nothing really works for him. Not at the office, not his friends, not even his girls." The future belongs to the "purblind, mating weasels" who "hold back" and believe that "being busy is the same thing as being alive." Down to humping his file clerks on the office floor, Maitland knows that no effort has any point; life is getting emptier by the minute: "the circle just seems to get smaller" and "the game isn't worth the candle." Maitland's fantasy defense gradually intrudes on his office routine as his grip on reality slips. Until, in a final unforgettable image, Maitland hangs up the phone (used throughout as an inventive symbol for his intensifying isolation) on his wife, his last link with humankind. Resigned to apartness, silence, and immobility, "he replaces the receiver and sits back waiting."

In Maitland's story Osborne judges modern life and finds that a process attributable to centuries of Protestant capitalism, but too far gone to be alleviated by knowledge of its cause, is almost at its end, our end. D. H. Lawrence described this paralysis perfectly forty years ago: "Most of the responses are dead, most of the awareness is dead, nearly all the constructive activity is dead, and all that remains is a sort of shell, a half-empty creature fatally self-preoccupied and incapable of either giving or taking. . . . Enclosed within the vicious circle of the self, with no vital contacts outside, the self becomes emptier and emptier, till it is almost a nullus, a nothingness." Omit the "almost" and we have Maitland, one of the most thoroughgoing pictures of pure desperation in recent drama, a mean bastard whose nothingness somehow touches us profoundly without exonerating his "irredeemable mediocrity." Like all plays that live, this one takes us out of ourselves for a time so that we might return to ask how *we* are living. As Jimmy Porter seems at times a representative dream figure expressing a lifetime of repressed anger against unspeakable humiliations, Maitland too is a dream-image repository for our innermost fear of self-diminishment, nonrecognition, and the loveless aloneness that prefigures death. But maybe we can still lay slight claim to Lawrence's "almost." This play gives us a chance to measure how much room we have left.

It is a critical commonplace that affluence took the sting out of Osborne's anger and that his work after *Inadmissible Evidence,* four plays in as many years, represents a steady, lamentable decline. True, a graph of Osborne's career plotted along a horizontal axis of chronological order and a vertical axis of artistic merit would be extremely jagged, with the last four plays decidedly on the downside of *Evidence.* But the later works themselves vary widely in quality and conclude not with an epitaph for John Osborne but on an upbeat note of promise.

A Patriot for Me (1965) suffers from the sheer largeness of its intent. Osborne so badly wanted to write a big play about big themes—homosexuality, corrupt society, the decay of civilization—that he ends up writing a very deliberate, stiff, and finally pompous play. While the subjects are dear to him, he confines them to a found, historical action rather than to one that surges irresistibly out of his own imagination. As in *A Subject of Scandal and Concern,* Osborne digs deeply into the byways of history to come up with a lonesome, tormented central figure whose personal troubles are interlocked with a sick whited-sepulchre society, once again distant in time and style but clearly standing for our own. *Patriot* tells, in twenty-three scenes, the story of Alfred Redl, an intelligence officer in turn-of-the century Vienna. The first half of the play is devoted to the painful emergence of Redl's homosexuality; the second is a dreary spy tale of blackmail, treason, exposure, and suicide. The homosexuality mentioned flippantly or seriously but peripherally in most of Osborne's plays is at the dead center of this one. In 1965 it was a daring theatrical breakthrough to present an unjudgmental treatment of a then *verboten* subject that still cannot be ignored by any writer trying to deal comprehensively with contemporary urban culture. Old hat in the theater now, the theme was threatening enough five years ago to prevent the play from getting the Lord Chamberlain's seal when Osborne refused to cut whole scenes, including the famous drag ball.

While the homosexual coming-out dominates *Patriot,* Osborne works along four other thematic and stylistic lines: a character study of a kind he hadn't done before, of a reticent, constrained, hidden (from himself and others) protagonist; an ironical portrait of mask and face, rule and misrule in a decadent imperialist society (revealed in the drag ball parody of the royal ball); a cinematic structure of rapid interplay between public and private scenes; and, in terms of point of view, a relentless camera-eye detachment of the sort he had begun to try in *Inadmissible Evidence.* But these strands never gel into the thoroughgoing ironic play Osborne intended; rather they freeze. *Patriot* is the coldest, most unrelaxed play Osborne has written, not only because Redl is tight and icy but because Osborne just doesn't known him from the inside out. Ibsen used to say that he wasn't ready to write a play until he could imagine what his characters would be wearing if they were to appear unexpectedly in his study. Osborne knows Jimmy, Archie, and Maitland that thoroughly. Redl remains a forced intellectual conception, as flat as a photographic image, unable to bear the thematic weight Osborne would have him carry.

I don't wish to leave the impression that *Patriot* has no redeeming virtues. The sexual tension of the opening scene is riveting, as are moments of insight into the despair and its attendant cruelty in the homosexual world. (Osborne's point is precisely that it is *the* world, and not a deviant subculture. Homosexuality and power are as symbiotically inseparable here as propriety and pornography in Victorian England.) Most of the dialogue is graceful; and the portrait of the military and aristocracy is suggestively handled. But these are little flickers of liveliness at the extremities of a play that never comes fully alive at its heart.

A Bond Honoured (1966), adapted from Lope de Vega's *La Fianza Satisfecha,* was commissioned by the National Theatre. While the original gives Osborne an opportunity to sketch in by far the angriest of his angry men, he is never comfortable with Lope's theological dialectic or his appraisal of the value system taken for granted by the aristocracy of the Spanish Golden Age. Osborne tries to turn Lope's sinning and repenting Leonido into something like an existentialist Lucifer, confronting his nothingness ("my life . . . is no more than fluff at the bottom of the pocket") by a satanic violation—evil be thou my good—of not only all the commandments but every human bond as well. He has raped and impregnated his mother, blinded his father, slept with his sister-daughter, and then tortured her because she refused to submit to him after her marriage. The best Osborne can do with this wholly alien material (not only do Christians and Moors clash onstage, but who ever expected Christ himself to show up in an Osborne play?) is struggle to make some kind of statement about the staggering inventory of violence festering in all of us. Leonido has marvelous untapped possibilities as a parody on Osborne-ism, taking as he does the traits of an Osborne protagonist to their ludicrous extremes: aliveness as value in a bland social matrix that rewards self-effacement; thwarted energy turned into neurotic destructiveness; asking too much from life and going under; intimate and long acquaintance with pain. And of course it is England that Leonido describes in his self-praise: "They were all consumed with process. Had no idea of the unique. Me, I had an overstrong instinct . . . and this is an island of over-protected people. The range of possibilities in living here shrinks every year. Soon it will be every week." Inexplicably, Osborne specifies that the play shall be acted Noh-style, with all the cast onstage throughout, getting up to do their scenes while the nonparticipants look on. This arbitrary staging is symptomatic of his awkwardness about what to do with the whole undertaking.

Osborne recently told an interviewer that "the theatre as I know it, and can work for it, has probably got a limited life. I think the literate theater of words and rounded psychological characterization is a decadent art form, like opera or ballet . . . and it's going to have a smaller and smaller audience . . . so I think I should go on with it while I can." In *Time Present* (1968), he makes this shrinking theater a major factor in the life of the actress Pamela Orme, his sole female protagonist. As her teen-age stepsister, a true child of the mixed media age, says: "Those draggy plays. Who wants them? . . . your scene is really out . . . and you with it." Pamela can only agree. At the present time, when everyone is in show biz, selling personality and cashing in on the latest popular tide, Pamela is an anachronism, an artist who tries to "give the audience the real thing sometimes." She chooses not to adjust to a world she despises, and the lack of creative release for "the best in her" twists her energy into a familiar Osborne personality: vituperative, haranguing, isolated, drifting, tense, bored, self-involved, disappointed with life, ungiving and unable to receive.

Despite sideswipes at modern rock culture and "peddling in the market place," the play zeros in on a nearly plotless character study of Pamela at a crisis point, before and after the off-stage death of her father, one of the last heroic actors of the Henry Irving variety. Pamela is a pallid version of Hedda Gabler, locked into an Electra relationship with an omnipotent, idealized, dead father whose grip on her psyche is so powerful that she cannot sustain any living connection. Gideon Orme has indoctrinated his daughter with a system of obsolete values of fineness and style in art and life, and a hatred of the vulgarity she sees everywhere. That is, he has rendered her unfit for compromise or "vulgar" commitment to an imperfect world. Osborne surrounds her with a contrasting set of characters—vulgar all—who are participating in life, groping toward the difficult "loving openness" that is our only way of "hoping to live in some sort of present." But Pamela is a sensitive hothouse plant violated by existence itself. At least she knows this, and, true to her unloving self, goes off into a permanent willed aloneness at the end. The trouble with the play is that we wave good riddance and don't care. Her story, unlike Bill Maitland's, is not presented as an explosion of forces boiling in all of us, and Osborne has not given her the bruised humanity of his other sick souls. We just don't feel that Pamela matters, that there is waste to regret.

Maybe this is the response Osborne seeks. The fact that he cannot (or will not?) squeeze a drop of sympathy out of us for Pamela suggests that for the first time in his plays he invites the audience to cool judgment of his central figure. Yet the play leaves the impression that it was written before Osborne was completely in control of his materials and of his attitudes toward his subject. There are a few teasing psychological insinuations of latent lesbianism and frigidity; we are unsure whether Pamela's choice is psychic rationalization or a heroic devotion to a dying art. I think a good deal of the fuzziness is attributable to Osborne's movement onto new moral ground that he doesn't yet firmly occupy. Pamela is no defender of values, no holdout against the decline of the West and the crushing of sensibility. In her final, calm acceptance of nothingness Osborne is showing the erosion of human richness through a kind of insane nonattachment. We have to live life now, for there has never been a static world that could accommodate yesteryear's romanticism. The price of disengagement (for any reason) is death-in-life, and it is too high even if one has to dirty one's hands in an unjust, tasteless society or yield the hoarded self in the quest for love. Passivity and protest, anger and letting life happen to us, aren't enough. The question Osborne begins to pose in *Time Present* is: how are we to save ourselves from ending up a Maitland or a Pamela?

That Osborne's outlook is changing is borne out by *The Hotel in Amsterdam* (1968), produced just two months after *Time Present*. Archie Rice said in his curtain number that "life . . . is like sucking a sweet with the wrapper on." In *The Hotel in Amsterdam* the hermetically sealed cellophane begins to open up and some of the flavor seeps through. Three couples, old friends, sneak away from their domineering boss (a movie mogul) for a precious weekend of mutal appreciation. That is almost all there is to the surface of the play—six people drinking and chatting with the directness, license, and tolerance of long friendship, "just us talking among ourselves." Osborne works with a very sharp and difficult formal idea, an attempt at a carefully orchestrated ensemble play which delicately, with no building crisis, reveals the quality of the lives of a close-knit nonfamilial group. With the exception of the few melodramatic touches he seems unable to avoid (the minimal plot unfolds with the help of the sudden appearance of an irrelevant character and the announcement of an offstage suicide), the form is the least forced slice-of-life Osborne has constructed.

His characters are representative of the upper middle class, early middle-aged urban lumpen intelligentsia: parents and spouses, successful journeymen workers in the commercial arts who know they produce a commodity and have no blazing vision to bestow upon the world. They are laboring to face without despair the meaninglessness of work after years of tense "making it"; the boredom of living, the wearing away of love, the aching loneliness in the middle of the night. The challenge is to stay open and vulnerable, to assimilate the "long process of disappointment" (as Osborne described life in an interview before the play premiered) into a deepening humanity. We cannot, like Pamela Orme, walk out on life (not for more than a weekend), and when Osborne's characters *do* in this play it is to steal a precious chance to rediscover what is truly valuable: the ongoing capacity to need others without shame, and those

[40]

cherished moments of at-oneness which renew our strength to survive the tears of things.

A new tone, emotional and dramaturgic, guides *The Hotel in Amsterdam*. To use a surprising word in connection with Osborne, one might even call the play gentle. The edge of his bitterness is blunted, more accepting of life's unfairness. For the first time he writes a play in which human misery ebbs as well as flows. To begin with, there is virtually no social commentary or class consciousness. Secondly, nothing very dramatic happens to any of the group—no hysterectomies, accidental pregnancies, sexual desperation, or crackups. To be sure, there is Osborne's ubiquitous grumbling character with an arm's length list of prejudices whose compulsive wit tends to take over stage center. But Laurie in this play is not merely a variation on an old theme. He is tempered by the ensemble intent and differs from earlier examples of his type in two significant respects: he likes everyone onstage, so that his invective is closer to harmless cocktail-party cleverness than to the sadism of Jimmy or Pamela; and more importantly, despite his self-pity and attention-getting devices, he is affectionate and can readily express admiration for others. Unlike other Osborne characters, he is not fiercely disintegrating; none of these people are.

The new emotional atmosphere is typified by a brief scene near the end in which two people, married but not to each other, confess their long-standing love. Nothing active will come of this admission, no affair and certainly no broken marriages. Nor do they have any illusion that a moment's connection can be extended into a lifetime's fulfillment. But both are richer for the acknowledgment of caring, and a little more alive, understanding, and giving. The play is concerned with renewal, not destruction. This scene captures the play's mood: a mixture of quiet sadness, wistful yearning, and an undefeated awareness of our creatureliness, of the absolute value of shared human experi-

[41]

ence. There is no god, there is no grandiose self-realization, but the alternative doesn't have to be nothingness. We make do with what we can do for each other. Perhaps we die alone and unsatisfied, but we don't have to suffer unto death convinced we are the butts of some cosmic joke which condemns us to revenge ourselves on ourselves. Cross over the mountain of anger and find not the promised land but other people and maybe a little love.

I don't mean to suggest that we should jump to the conclusion that Osborne's humanity has fully matured, nor that his character drawing has advanced into a radiant optimism. On the contrary, he is far from at ease with either this new quietness of feeling or the static, tranquil structure. The play suffers in dramatic interest from the absence of both savage indignation and the passion of stark failure. In attempting to de-emphasize the heights and depths of feeling, Osborne flattens his emotional planes (and his characterization) so uniformly that there is a certain dullness in the play's progress. Yet there is a fascination in watching Osborne changing as a dramatist, trying to abandon what comes naturally and to write a new kind of play, one without emptiness or loss at its center. And, as always in his better work, there is plenty of opportunity for us to undergo the comfort and shock of recognizing ourselves.

Unlike so many of his characters, John Osborne is decidedly not, to quote Pamela Orme's self-summation, "stuck." He is often accused of being a Johnny One-Note able to hit only the shrill high C of anger. But this play and *Time Present* show that his value system, as well as his craft, is in considerable flux. Life remains basically "pain, absurdity, distress," but largely gone are the demands for pure sincerity in relationships, the hate letters to society, the crabby nastiness of failure and disillusioned idealism, and much of the psychological violence. Beginning to emerge are the softer values previously crushed by the sheer unfairness of things: gentleness, charity, decency, trust, love.

Not that the world has improved, or Osborne mellowed. As the main character in his next play points out, Osborne's unmerry England is yet a place, like Yeats's Ireland, of "great hatred, little room." But the social situation is dismissed in a phrase or two in *The Hotel in Amsterdam;* its awfulness so entrenched it can be taken for granted. It is a fact of life to be lived with, not consumed by. Osborne can now place a wholly new emphasis on the process of "hoping to live in some sort of present." Thus, while "dread" is "still never very far away" from the uneasy reconciliations of *The Hotel in Amsterdam,* Osborne lets his people live with the dependencies and self-deceptions, with whatever it takes to keep going, that he had stripped from all his characters right up to Pamela. The imagination of disaster begins to shade into an intimation of troubled survival.

It would be pleasing to close this study on a note of continuing movement and change, to report a deepening of the muted chord of hope sounded in *The Hotel in Amsterdam* or Osborne's increasing mastery of that play's ensemble method. But the struggle for love and imperfect survival has yielded in his recent work to older feelings of despair, to the enduring boredom, helplessness, and unkindness that are the familiar signposts of Osborne's world. Stillborn were the softness and the compassionate regret that allowed for moments of true connection, if only in shared disappointment. Osborne has returned to the theme of psychic annihilation. The desperate myth of the Pamelas and Maitlands is ascendant once more, intensified in his latest work to a nightmarish vision of the arrival of pure chaos.

Since *The Hotel in Amsterdam* Osborne has written two competent but unexceptional television plays, a severely flawed full-length play and an adaptation of *Hedda Gabler.* The first of the TV pieces, *The Right Prospectus* (1970), is offbeat Osborne; one has to go as far back as *Under Plain Cover* to find a similar playfulness of imagination that thoroughly ignores realistic conventions. The scene is an English boys' public school. A middle-aged couple, financially successful, have decided to return to complete their interrupted education. In a *Zero for Conduct* kind of fantasy, they are treated exactly like other pupils, with no sex or age differences. The husband fails dismally; the wife triumphs radiantly. The free-flowing montage style provides a clever, ironic way of revealing the winner-loser characters of the couple and offers occasions for predictable sniping at public school snobbishness. The play is Osborne's least thematically ambitious; it is nothing more than a witty but unchallenging entertainment.

The next of the TV plays, *Very Like a Whale* (1971), is a throwback to the standard Osborne portrait of irreversible disintegration. Sir Jock Mellor, captain of industry, is presented in the last weeks of his life, soon after he is knighted for his contributions to industrial technology. However, his work is meaningless to him, his marriage futile, his children unable to salve his heart's pain. In a rapid series of sketchy vignettes, we are shown Sir Jock's recognition of his uselessness to himself or his family as he dwindles inexorably toward a lonely death. The theme is quintessential Osborne, but handled so slightly that the play seems no more than a notebook entry, a five finger exercise (after the fact) for a major work like *Inadmissible Evidence.* The question is why would Osborne bother doing something so miniature that he had done to perfection long before?

West of Suez (1971), Osborne's most recent original work for the Royal Court, is an ill-made play of substantial but largely unrealized seriousness. Its themes are Osborne's trademarks: the self-consummation of the old, fetid English social order; the importance of doing real work like writing that is no mere capitulation to the plastic wasteland of technology but is wrought out of dangerous combat with the naked self; and, above all, the suffering unto death of what Beckett calls the "balls-aching boredom" of life's long process of disappointment. Set on a formerly colonial Caribbean island, the play begins promisingly in the slow, unclimactic lifelike groupings of *The Hotel in Amsterdam.* We meet the vacationing family of the famous, aging writer Wyatt Gillman as they "observe one another and speculate and chatter on." Working again with ensemble groupings, Osborne gradually reveals his characters' intelligence and purposeless energy and the "vague pain" of a lifetime of unsatisfied yearning. They do not recognize or, if they do, cannot express the fact that this yearning is for love. So they are a typical gallery of Osborne people: frustrated, defensive, guilt-plagued, hostile, too sensitive and complex to live unsullied by life's daily degradation, their humanity as well as their anguish stemming from their unfillable demands on life. Through the rhythms and innuendoes of the ensemble structure, Osborne builds up considerable dramatic and psychological interest in the egocentric father's effect on his daughters. But then, midway through the second act, Osborne wrenches the play into a very clumsy symbolic mode. The Gillman family suddenly becomes representative of the last remnants of colonial England (which has been dying piecemeal since the Suez crisis) about to be pitilessly exterminated by young revolutionaries and angry natives. We are jolted from the impressionistic, Chekhov-like form into no less than a visionary allegory of apocalypse. In *The Entertainer* Osborne had brilliantly built the political level organically into the music hall framework so that his characters *embodied* history. In *West of Suez* the connection is unprepared for and arbitrary. Aiming at revelation, Osborne manages only confusion.

History is ever ironical, and fifteen years after *Look Back in Anger* we find Osborne celebrating the Gillmans, despite their cruelty and impotence, as the final humane generation and condemning the word-hating, narcissistic younger generation as the new fascism. (Osborne's blanket denunciation of youth is startling and unpleasant.) At the end of *West of Suez* the rough beast has sprung and the future belongs not to meek socialist

[45]

men of decency and charity, the beautiful losers like Jimmy Porter, but to the undiscriminatingly violent. Osborne intends an overwhelming image of stark horror, of the absolute perplexity of his (and my) generation face to face with "all this desolation we live in." It is an urgent theme. In *West of Suez* he fails to give it dramatic life, but at least he is struggling with it, plunging as always unhesitatingly to the core of our most immediate anxieties.

Looking over Osborne's sixteen plays and remembering that he probably has more playwriting years ahead of him than behind, what evaluation is useful? He has written no unflawed play and a cluster of bad ones — at least five. They are just *there*, and no amount of critical dodging ("if he hadn't gotten these out of his system, he wouldn't have had the inspiration for those") or authorial rationalization ("artists should have the right to relax . . . to indulge themselves") can disguise them. Nor would he rank high on the list of contemporary writers one would turn to for intellectual stimulation. Osborne is no playwright of ideas; his thought is easily compressible into a simple statement of experience-oriented humanist existentialism. All of his work, good or bad, is urgent, passionate, and deliberately anti-intellectual. Philosophy is embedded in behavior and affect usually organized into an action of increasing isolation of a main character. And he has had no lasting effect on dramatic form. I must admit to frequent bafflement in trying to mobilize the tools of my trade — an exhaustive training in structural methodology — to deal with Osborne. He offers nearly none of the mythical density or intricate poetic patterning of a Beckett, Pinter, or Genet to test analytic ingenuity. His demands, rather, are almost solely on the store of our human sympathy. He always works in terms of immediate feeling and response, willing to risk a fall into sentimentality in order to gain a fierce truthfulness to "the burden of living" and "the texture of ordinary despair." This is another way of saying that he is essentially a man of the theater, particularly of an actor's theater. Undiminished is his amazing gift for creating magnificent roles that have been graced by some of the great performances of our time. And, although he has not written at the top of his talent for eight years, he remains the *exciting* dramatist he so brilliantly began as. Exciting because three times—in *Look Back in Anger, The Entertainer,* and *Inadmissible Evidence*—he has articulated as fully as any writer the central experience of his age. We look forward to his doing this again, anticipating that each next play might gather masses of the unclear feeling of these complicated times and help us to a harrowing revelation of the way we are living.

SELECTED BIBLIOGRAPHY

Works of John Osborne

Look Back in Anger. London, Faber & Faber, 1957.

The Entertainer. London, Faber & Faber, 1957.

Epitaph for George Dillon (in collaboration with Anthony Creighton). London, Faber & Faber, 1958.

The World of Paul Slickey. London Faber & Faber, 1959.

A Subject of Scandal and Concern. London, Faber & Faber, 1961.

Luther. London, Faber & Faber, 1963.

Plays for England. London, Faber & Faber, 1963.

Tom Jones: A Screenplay. London, Faber & Faber, 1964; revised ed., New York, Grove Press, 1964.

Inadmissible Evidence. London, Faber & Faber, 1965.

A Patriot for Me. London, Faber & Faber, 1966.

A Bond Honoured. London, Faber & Faber, 1966.

Time Present and The Hotel in Amsterdam. London, Faber & Faber, 1968.

The Right Prospectus: A Play for Television. London, Faber & Faber, 1970.

West of Suez. London, Faber & Faber, 1971.

Very Like a Whale. London, Faber & Faber, 1971.

Hedda Gabler by Henrik Ibsen: Adapted by John Osborne. London, Faber & Faber, 1972.

Critical Works and Commentary

Banham, Martin. Osborne. Edinburgh, Oliver & Boyd, 1969.

Carter, Alan. John Osborne. Edinburgh, Oliver & Boyd, 1969.

Corrigan, Robert. "The Drama of the Disengaged Man," in The New Theatre of Europe, 3. New York, Delta Books, 1968.

Hayman, Ronald. John Osborne. London, Heinemann, 1968.

Lahr, John. "John Osborne: Poor Johnny One-Note," in Up Against the Fourth Wall. New York, Grove Press, 1970.

Mander, John. "Art and Anger," in The Writer and Commitment. London, Secker & Warburg, 1961.

Marowitz, Charles, Tom Milne, and Owen Hale. The Encore Reader. London, Methuen, 1965.

Taylor, John Russell. Anger and After. London, Methuen, 1962.

—— Look Back in Anger: A Casebook. London, Macmillan, 1968.

Trussler, Simon. The Plays of John Osborne. London, Gollancz, 1969.

Williams, Raymond. "Recent English Drama," in The Pelican Guide to English Literature, 7. Middlesex, Pelican, 1967.